MAGIC

FOR KIDS

FAY PRESTO

MAGIC

FOR KIDS

NEW YORK

KINGFISHER
Larousse Kingfisher Chambers Inc.
95 Madison Avenue
New York, New York 10016

First published in 1999

2 4 6 8 10 9 7 5 3 1

1TR/0599/HY/MAR(MAR)/128TPMA

LIBRARY OF CONGRESS CATALOGING-IN-PUBLICATION DATA
Presto, Fay.
Magic for kids / by Fay Presto.—1st ed.
p. cm.
Summary: Text and step-by-step photographic sequences explain how
to do a variety of magic tricks, including sleight of hand tricks,
rope tricks, illusions, and more.
1. Magic tricks Juvenile literature.   [1. Magic tricks.]
I. Title.
GV1548.P72   1999
793.8—dc21   99–12753   CIP

ISBN 0-7534-5210-3

Printed in Hong Kong

Senior editor: Sarah Milan
Senior designer: Sarah Goodwin
Production controller: Caroline Jackson
Photographer: Ray Moller
Illustrator: Woody

INTRODUCTION

Hello! My name is Fay Presto. For the last 16 years, I have been having a lot of fun performing magic. One day, after I had been doing some very boring jobs, I decided I would really like to be a magician. So I bought some books about magic, put an act together, and off I went. On the way, I discovered some important things: magic is easier than you might think it is; it's not just about tricks, but about people and how you get along with them; and it is about how you present yourself. This book has many new tricks to learn, but it also tells you how to present them, how to present yourself, and how to put on a show. It's hard to feel confident about performing if you haven't done it before. The only way to conquer your fear is to get out there and perform! Magic has been good to me—I have traveled around the world and met many interesting people. And if I've done a particularly good show, I've been rewarded with that most wonderful thing—applause! I hope this book will help you get started in the world of entertainment, whether you put on a few tricks for some friends or use it as a first step to a glittering career.

Fay Presto

CONTENTS

HOW TO USE THIS BOOK

 Learn to recognize the features explained below. They have been designed to help you find your way easily around the pages that introduce new tricks and techniques (pages 16–65).

This symbol indicates how easy or difficult the trick is to learn and perform.

easy **medium** **difficult**

The introductory text explains what the audience will see. It also tells the magician whether a second person is needed to help with the performance.

The Tips box gives one or two useful hints that the magician should keep in mind when preparing or performing the trick.

The heading SETUP introduces the steps that the magician must take immediately before the performance. They should be read after the PREPARATION section.

---

60   Anyone Home?

ANYONE HOME?

 Here is a dramatic trick that works well if there is a lot of space between you and the audience. You will need a small, but cooperative assistant—a younger sister or brother, maybe—and you will need to spend time preparing the main prop—the house from which they will appear.

PREPARATION

YOU WILL NEED:
• a large cardboard box
• a pair of strong scissors
• glue
• colored cardboard or paint

Tips
When putting on a show, do this as an opening trick—little people can't sit still for long!

SETUP
1 Get your assistant to sit quietly under the table before anyone comes into the room. There should be a long tablecloth over the table, so she cannot be seen.

2 Place the roof right next to one side of the table, and put the main part of the house anywhere nearby.

PERFORMANCE
1 Pick up the house and show everyone that it is empty. Then put it down beside of the roof. There should be no space between the roof, the house, and the table.

2 Walk to the front of the stage and keep talking to your audience about what you are going to do next. Meanwhile, your assistant crawls from under the table, behind the roof, and through the secret door into the house. She must be very careful not to move the house as she does this.

The heading PREPARATION is followed by a YOU WILL NEED box, which lists everything needed for the trick. This in turn is followed by several steps showing how to make or prepare your props. The section headed PREPARATION should be read before going on to SETUP.

This symbol indicates whether the trick is best performed in close-up, as a floor show, or on a stage.

close-up

floor show

stage

In the PREPARATION section, numbered steps explain how to prepare the props needed for the trick. Each step is clearly illustrated.

Under the heading PERFORMANCE, are the steps that the magician has to do to perform the trick. Each step is clearly numbered and explained. The steps are also illustrated with photographs.

The Patter box contains suggested patter, or talk, that the magician can use throughout the trick. Where the text is interrupted by three dots, this means the patter has moved on to the next step of the performance.

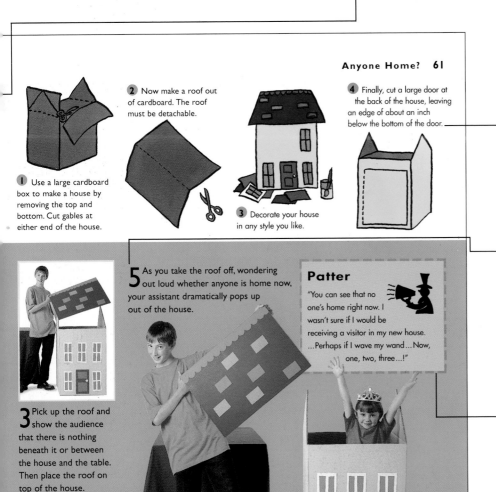

Anyone Home?   61

2 Now make a roof out of cardboard. The roof must be detachable.

4 Finally, cut a large door at the back of the house, leaving an edge of about an inch below the bottom of the door.

1 Use a large cardboard box to make a house by removing the top and bottom. Cut gables at either end of the house.

3 Decorate your house in any style you like.

5 As you take the roof off, wondering out loud whether anyone is home now, your assistant dramatically pops up out of the house.

Patter

"You can see that no one's home right now. I wasn't sure if I would be receiving a visitor in my new house. ...Perhaps if I wave my wand...Now, one, two, three...!"

3 Pick up the roof and show the audience that there is nothing beneath it or between the house and the table. Then place the roof on top of the house.

4 You now say a few magic words or wave your wand.

USEFUL TIPS

The time will come when you are ready to put on your own show. Before you throw yourself into your act, take some time to read the information on the next few pages. One of the secrets of being a successful magician is to learn the tricks of the trade—discovered the hard way by magicians before you!

THINGS TO REMEMBER

On most pages of this book there are Tips boxes. These contain useful information to help you with a particular trick. On the next six pages, there are other general tips and hints that you should try to remember while practicing and performing magic.

SMOOTH OPERATOR

When you watch someone perform magic well, it seems as if everything is so easy. In fact, the magician's brain is probably racing, figuring out which trick to do next, how much more the audience wants, and how to get the trick they're doing to work properly! Try to stay calm on the outside, even if you can't be calm on the inside.

IT'S SHOWTIME!

Whenever and wherever you perform tricks, you are putting on a *show*. Whether it is on stage at a school concert or at the table after dinner, you'll need to give your show some shape by planning a beginning, a middle, and an end.

LOCATION

Take a few minutes to look at the area where you will be performing. Many rooms have a natural focus. This might be a fireplace, a corner, or a door. When you have the exact spot, tailor your routine accordingly. The symbols in this book will help you decide whether a particular trick is suitable for a close-up, floor show, or stage setting. The location should be the key to which tricks you choose.

Make sure your props, including tables and chairs, are in place before you start.

SEQUENCE

The sequence of tricks you put on in your show is important. You may want to perform one trick in which some silks appear magically from a box, then plan to use these same silks for the next trick. Always finish on a dramatic note, so that you leave your audience wanting more!

DON'T TELL

Never repeat a trick, no matter how tempting it may be. The second time around, your audience will be looking for the secret behind your act. No matter how hard you try, you won't be able to impress them in the same way as you did the first time. You should also resist the temptation to tell people the secret of how a trick is done. They will only be disappointed that the magic can be explained away.

DIVERT ATTENTION

If you want to do something without the audience noticing, ask a question. They will automatically look at your face, not at your hands, and you can quickly work some clever magic.

PRACTICE YOUR TECHNIQUE

Remember that practice makes perfect. Use a mirror to see how the tricks will appear to your audience. If you still feel unsure, you can try out a trick on one or two good friends.

ENJOY YOURSELF!

Even though you will be thinking about several different things at the same time, remember that the object of putting on a magic show is for you and the audience to have fun. Of course, you should concentrate on what you're doing, but remember to enjoy yourself too—the rest will follow naturally.

Use a mirror to show yourself what the audience will see.

ACT THE PART

When you are putting on a show, you'll find that it helps put yourself and your audience in the right mood if you act the part of a convincing magician. A successful performance is all about presentation—knowing how to act and what to say—so it is worth spending time thinking about the type of magician you want to be.

SPARKLY OR SOLEMN?

Are you a bit of a clown? Well, why not bring out that side of you and dress up as a funny character, cracking jokes to go with your tricks. Or maybe you're the quiet type? In that case, you could put on a more mysterious act, performing your tricks against a background of spooky music. After all, it's easier to be who you really are than to try to be someone very different on stage. On the other hand, you may *prefer* to be someone different from your usual self—it's up to you.

Simple and elegant can be highly effective.

DRESSING UP

When you've decided what kind of character you'd like to be, it helps to have a costume. This could be a clown's baggy pants and red nose, a top hat and cape with stars on it, or a fairy costume. Or it may just be a special jacket or dress that you only wear for performances.

BE PRACTICAL

Don't forget that whatever you choose to wear, for some tricks you will need a costume with long sleeves in which to hide props. Pockets can come in handy for holding coins and other small objects. But make sure the costume isn't so fussy or complicated that it gets in your way and distracts you from the real business of performing magic.

WHERE TO PERFORM

Think about where you are going to perform. If you're going to be doing something at the table after dinner, it might look silly if you rush off to put on a sparkly cape and hat. If you are entertaining at a school concert, it is a compliment to your audience to take a little trouble with what you wear. If you *look* a little special, it is much easier to *be* a little special.

You can rent colorful and flamboyant costumes for that extra-special occasion.

PATTER MATTERS

"Patter" is the type of conversation or chatter that magicians and other entertainers often use while they are performing. You'll find it's a good idea to develop some patter of your own, partly to explain to the audience what you're doing (or what you want them to think you're doing!) and partly to keep them from watching you too closely during the tricky parts of your performance. You will find "Patter" boxes like the one above with every trick in this book. They can be used as a guide to help you perform.

Patter

"Hello, everybody. I'm the friendly wiz that is."

"Good afternoon, ladies and gentlemen. I'm going to try a few experiments with a deck of cards."

"Is it here, is it there? I'd love to know, it isn't fair."

"Now you see it, now you don't. No point in asking, 'cause tell you, I won't."

"I've got a little something to show you. It could be lots of fun. Keep your eyes wide open to figure out how it's done!"

KEEP PRACTICING

It takes some time to be able to talk easily at the same time as you perform a trick—especially one that requires a lot of dexterity. By practicing your patter with the easier tricks first, you'll soon be able to do this during more difficult ones.

PROPS AND PUPPETS

The pieces of equipment used by magicians as part of their act are known as props—short for theatrical properties. The simpler ones can be found around the house or borrowed from the audience. Others can be specially prepared ahead of time or bought from magic stores.

TYPES OF PROPS

Most magicians perform with the help of props. These include everyday objects like a deck of cards, pieces of rope, or coins. They can also be objects that look ordinary but aren't, and these need to be either homemade or bought. Cardboard boxes with false bottoms or secret doors, tubes with hidden compartments, and containers that use secret mirrors are examples of these.

MAGIC SHOPS

Other props, such as extra-large playing cards, magic wands, and magician's silks can all be bought at special magic stores. (See page 71). If normal playing cards are too big for your hands, you can buy smaller cards from these stores, too.

Extra-large cards can be found in magic shops.

CAN I BORROW A...?

Some of the most effective props are things that the magician "borrows" from members of the audience, such as coins or bills. Or—if the magician is putting on a show during a meal—things that he or she picks up from the table, such as a napkin, a saltshaker, or a glass. By using objects that are at hand, it seems to the audience that the magician has not had time to prepare the props or to do anything secret with them—and the apparent spontaneity will add to the realism of the performance. On top of this, the audience won't be suspicious of the props themselves. After all, how can they mistrust something that came from their own back pocket?

MAKE YOUR OWN PROPS

Some of the tricks in this book require home-made props. Each of these has clear instructions on how it is made and what equipment you need.

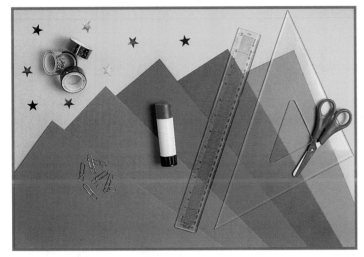

Decorate the props you make with colored paper, shiny tape, and stick-on shapes.

For most of them, all you need are inexpensive, easy-to-find objects, such as dishwashing liquid bottles, cardboard boxes, margarine tubs, and empty matchboxes. Each step is clearly explained and illustrated under the heading PREPARATION.

You will need the following:
- a pencil
- a ruler
- scissors
- a triangle
- glue
- tape
- colored paper
- paint

and the world of magic is at your fingertips!

MAGIC WITH PUPPETS

Another type of prop that you may want to bring into your act, once you are confident about doing the tricks, is a hand puppet. These can only be used with certain kinds of tricks, where you won't be held back by the use of only one hand. But it can be helpful, as well as fun, to have a character on stage with you to talk to, to help you overcome your stage fright, or simply to make the trick look more effective.

Tricks you can perform with a puppet:
- Number Crunching
- Showing a Profit
- I Can Read You
- That's News to Me!
- Rope Through You
- Water Surprise
- Magical Tube
- Flat Top, Round Top
- Twice as Rice
- Busted Banana
- Glass Magic
- Ice Cream Queen
- Mirror Box
- Up Your Nose!
- Anyone Home?
- Get Lost!

NUMBER CRUNCHING

A member of the audience is asked to write down a series of numbers. When these are added up, they equal a prediction that you have already sealed in an envelope.

PREPARATION

YOU WILL NEED:
- a piece of paper
- a pen
- an envelope

SETUP

1 On a piece of paper, write down the four-figure number that is twice the current year's date, e.g.:
1999 = 3998
2000 = 4000

2 Seal the paper in the envelope. This is your prediction.

Patter

"In here is the sum of some numbers we haven't added up yet....Write the answers to some questions....Funny, our totals are the same!"

PERFORMANCE

1 Ask a helper to write down the year he was born. (This can be done on a flipchart for a floor show.)

3 Open the envelope. His total is the same as the number you have already written and sealed there.

2 Below this, he writes the year of an important event in his life, the age he is, or will be, on his birthday this year, and the number of years that have passed since the important event. Finally, he writes the total of these four numbers.

SHOWING A PROFIT

Six coins are placed on the page of a large dictionary, opened at the word "profit." You lift up the dictionary, sliding the coins into a helper's hands. But when he counts them, he finds there are ten—he has made a profit of four!

PREPARATION

YOU WILL NEED:
- a large dictionary with a sewn binding
- ten small coins

SETUP

Slide four coins into the spine of an open dictionary. Experiment first to make sure the binding is loose enough for the coins to slide out, but not so loose that they fall out.

Patter

"They always said that if I became a good magician, I could make a profit. Let's turn to the word "profit".... Here we are. Now, put these six coins in the book...close it...think about money. Now open it....How's that for a return!"

PERFORMANCE

1 Open the dictionary at the page with the word "profit." Give your helper six coins and ask him to put them on the open page along the center crease.

2 Close the book and wave your magic wand over it.

3 Open the book at the same page and lift it up so that the coins fall into your helper's hands.

4 Ask your helper to count the coins. He will be amazed to find that there are now ten.

I CAN READ YOU

In this trick, the audience chooses a page number from a book you have apparently chosen at random from the shelves. You leave the room while a helper reads the top line of the page aloud. When you come back into the room, you can "read" everyone's mind by revealing the top line.

PREPARATION

YOU WILL NEED:
- two identical books (dictionaries are best)
- a bookshelf or a pile of other books

SETUP

1 Set up the room with a shelf of books. Put one of the books you will be using on the shelf.

2 Hide the other identical book outside the room.

Patter

"Pick a page number in this book.... It's important that I don't see or hear what you choose, so I'll go outside....Concentrate hard....I'm getting it. It is..."

PERFORMANCE

1 Take a book off the shelf "at random" and hand it to a helper. Ask him and the audience to agree on a page number.

2 Now leave the room. While you are outside, your helper reads the top line of the agreed page aloud.

3 Meanwhile, look up the top line of the agreed page in the book you have hidden.

4 When you return, ask the audience to concentrate on the words, then slowly pretend to read their mind by revealing what was written.

THAT'S NEWS TO ME!

 In this trick, you cut a strip of newspaper at a point decided on by the audience and a helper. When you open a sealed envelope, the words written on the paper inside are the same as those on the top line of the newspaper at the point where it was cut.

PREPARATION

YOU WILL NEED:
- a newspaper
- scissors
- a piece of paper
- a pen
- an envelope

SETUP

1 Cut a strip of continuous text from a newspaper.

2 Clearly write the top line of this text on a piece of paper and seal it in an envelope.

Patter

"I have a strip of newspaper. Where would you like me to cut it? Say 'stop' at any time....Would you mind picking up that piece for me.... Read the top line aloud....That's what it says in here, too!"

PERFORMANCE

1 Hold the strip of newspaper upside down (far enough away from your helper so he can't see that it's upside down). Run the scissors up and down and ask your helper to say "stop" at any point.

2 Cut the strip at the point your helper indicates, and let the bottom part flutter onto the table or the floor.

3 Ask your helper to pick up the piece that has fallen. While he does this, turn the piece in your hand right side up.

4 Ask your helper to read aloud the top line of text from the piece he has picked up. Now bring out the envelope—sealed inside are the same words!

ROPE THROUGH YOU

This is a simple and effective trick for a floor show or stage performance. You will need to call on a volunteer. The audience sees you bring two pieces of rope around the back of your helper and then tie them loosely together at the front. You give both ends a sharp tug and the ropes appear to pass right through the helper's body.

PREPARATION

YOU WILL NEED:
- two pieces of rope, exactly the same length
- a short piece of thread

PERFORMANCE

1 Holding the two ropes in one hand to hide the tie, tell the audience you will pass two pieces of rope through your helper.

2 Bring the ropes around your helper's waist, keeping the tie out of sight behind his back.

3 Tie the ropes in a loose knot around your helper's waist, but be careful not to pull too hard when you do this.

SETUP

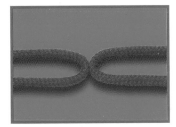

Fold the ropes in half and tie the loops together with a piece of thread. Give the loops a gentle tug to make sure the thread holds.

Patter

"I've been told that real magicians can saw people in half. I don't need all that expensive equipment—I can do it with two pieces of rope....Can I have a volunteer? Don't be scared, it won't hurt...much! There we are, not too tight, I hope?...My helper is now surrounded by two rings of the ropes of terror!...Abracadabra, he's free....You were inside these loops! Don't bend over too quickly for a week or so!"

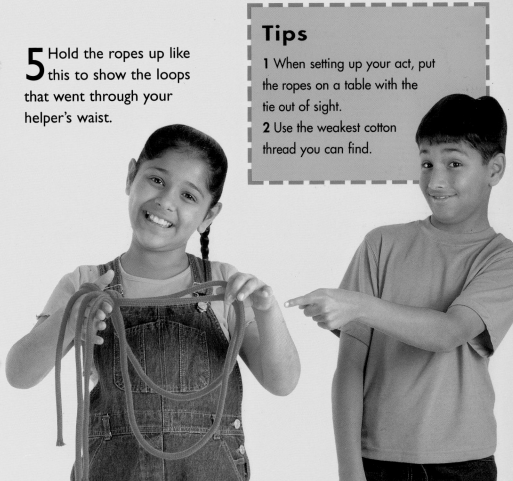

5 Hold the ropes up like this to show the loops that went through your helper's waist.

Tips

1 When setting up your act, put the ropes on a table with the tie out of sight.
2 Use the weakest cotton thread you can find.

4 Now tug the ends of the rope sharply to break the thread. The two pieces of ropes appear to go right through your helper!

ROPE WRIGGLER

In this trick, the audience sees you take three pieces of rope—one short, one medium length, and one long—and transform them into three pieces of rope, all of the same length. To get an idea of what the audience will see, practice this effect in front of a mirror.

PREPARATION

YOU WILL NEED:
- a long piece of rope
- scissors
- tape to stop the rope from fraying (optional)

PERFORMANCE

1 With the back of your hand toward the audience, hold the three pieces of rope next to each other in your left hand (if you are right-handed). Hold them between your thumb and index finger, with the top edges sticking up about 1½ in. above your hand.

2 With the back of your hand still facing the audience, take the bottom end of the short rope and put it next to the top end of the long rope.

3 Twist the bottom end of the short rope over the top of the top end of the long rope with your thumb. Make sure no one sees you do this.

4 Now take the bottom end of the medium rope and put it next to the other four ends. Take the bottom end of the long rope and put it next to the other five ends.

1 Cut the rope into three pieces: 10 in., 22 in., and 34 in. long.

2 Put some tape around the ends to keep them from fraying.

Tips

To add an extra element at the end of this trick, gather the ropes into a bundle and give them to a helper. Ask him or her to hand you back one piece of rope at a time. It will look as if the helper has changed the rope back to pieces of three different lengths.

5 Keeping the three ends of rope that are closest to your palm in your left hand, take the other three ends in your right hand.

6 Now pull your hands slowly apart, making sure the loop in your left hand is still hidden.

Patter

"In my hand I have three pieces of rope, each one a different length. I am going to bring the end of this rope up into my hand....Now, the ends of the next two ropes....Can everyone see?

For my next show, I need three pieces of rope all the same length, so why not transform them now?...I'll take hold of the three ends in one hand and three ends in another, pull them gently apart...three identical pieces!"

7 Drop the three ends held in your right hand, and show the audience that all three pieces of rope are the same length.

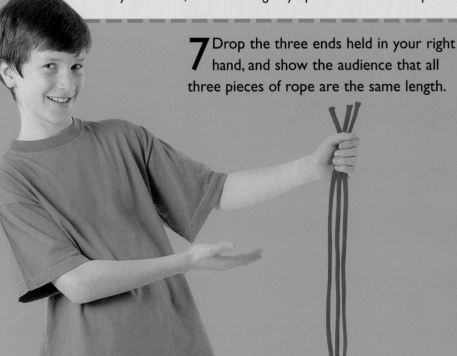

WATER SURPRISE

This trick is performed in several stages. First, you pour plain water through two empty tubes into a mug. You then throw the contents of the mug over the audience—but nothing comes out! You pour the contents of the tubes into a glass and out comes the water—but it has changed color!

PREPARATION

YOU WILL NEED:
- a plastic cup
- a paper clip
- two pieces of construction paper about 10 in. wide and 12 in. long
- tape
- scissors
- food coloring
- a glass or other transparent container
- a pitcher
- a mug or cup (this should not be transparent)

SETUP

1 Put a drop of food coloring into the plastic cup.

2 Slide the plastic cup inside the top of the smaller tube. Slide the larger tube over the top and hook the cup over both tubes with the paper clip. Make sure the cup is not visible.

PERFORMANCE

1 With your thumb covering the outside of the paper clip, slide out the inside tube with your left hand. The plastic cup should still be hooked to the outside tube.

2 Show the audience that the inside tube is empty. Hold the other tube toward you so that they can't see the cup.

3 Replace the inside tube by sliding it up from underneath. Now slide the outside tube off the bottom, making sure the cup is hooked to the inside tube.

4 This time, show that the outside tube is empty. Remember, hold the other tube so that they can't see the cup.

1 Cut off the rim of the plastic cup. Then, straighten the paper clip and tape it to the side of the cup.

2 Wrap a piece of construction paper, about 10 in. wide and 12 in. long, around the outside of the cup.

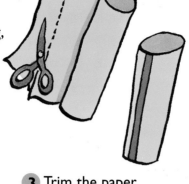

3 Trim the paper, leaving an overlapping edge of 2 inches, and tape the paper down the side to make a tube.

4 With the other piece of paper, make a second tube slightly wider than the first (the first tube must be able to slide inside the second tube.) Decorate the outside of both tubes.

5 Put the tubes back together again with the cup inside.

6 Holding the tubes above a mug, pour some water from a pitcher through the tubes into the mug. (The water actually goes into the plastic cup.)

7 Now pretend to throw the mug of water at the audience! (Option: have the mug filled with confetti to throw at them.)

8 Wave your wand over the tubes, then turn them upside down and pour the contents of the plastic cup into the empty glass. The water that appears in the glass has changed color!

Patter

"Two pretty tubes, both of them empty....
Now, I'll pour water through them into a mug.... See for yourselves!...
Amazing—the tubes have turned the water green!"

MAGICAL TUBE

You've seen it done before and now you, too, will be able to perform this classic trick. Your audience will see you pull several silk scarves out of an empty tube. This is a good trick that is not difficult to prepare or perform.

PREPARATION

YOU WILL NEED:
- an empty dishwashing liquid bottle
- a paper or plastic cup
- black paint
- a paintbrush
- scissors
- glue
- decorative paper or colored paint
- three or four colored silks

1 Cut off both ends of the dishwashing liquid bottle so that it becomes a tube.

2 Cut off about ¼ in. from the bottom of the cup. (You may need to cut off some more after you have done Step 3.)

3 Place the cup upside down inside the tube, just below the tube's rim. You may need to trim the top of the cup if it is too wide.

4 Paint the insides of both the tube and the cup black, then leave them to dry.

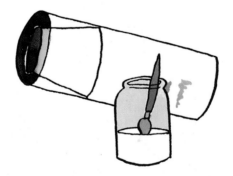

5 Put glue on the outside rim of the cup, then put it back inside the tube so that it sticks firmly.

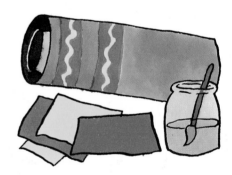

6 Finally, you can decorate the outside of your magical tube with colored paper or paint.

SETUP

1 Tie the colored silks together.

2 Wind the silks around the top end of the tube, tucking them into the gap between the edge of the cup and the tube so that they cannot be seen from the outside.

PERFORMANCE

1 Before picking up the tube to show that it is empty, pull out one end of the silk very slightly and hide it beneath your thumb.

2 Show the "empty" tube to the audience.

3 Wave your wand or sprinkle fairy dust over the tube and say a few magic words.

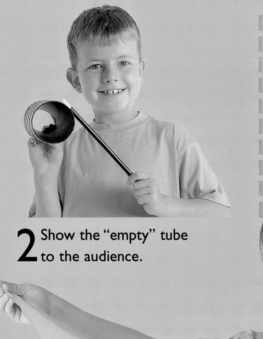

4 Now pull the silks dramatically out of the tube by transferring the tube to your other hand while still holding on to the silk that was hidden beneath your thumb.

FLAT TOP, ROUND TOP

This is an easy trick that will have your friends and family amazed at your powers of mind reading. You will be able to pick out the cards that two people have chosen from a deck. All it takes is a little practice in the art of telling two types of cards apart.

PREPARATION

YOU WILL NEED:
- a deck of cards

To do this trick, you have to learn to tell apart two different types of cards—those with numbers or letters that have a round top, and those that have a flat (or a sharp) top. 3, 5, 7, and K are flat; 4 and A are sharp. Look at the examples on the right. With practice, it'll get easier to spot which is which.

FLAT (OR SHARP) TOP
3 4 5 7 J K A
ROUND TOP
2 6 8 9 10 Q

SETUP

1 Sort the deck into two halves, one half consisting of round-topped cards and the other of flat- (or sharp-) top cards.

2 Now put the two halves back together. (With practice, you'll be able to sort the cards quickly in front of your audience.)

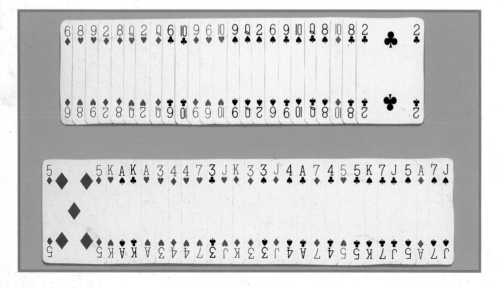

Patter

"I'm going to do a trick so powerful that I won't even touch the cards. Can I have two willing volunteers? Thank you. Now, each of you hold out your deck to the other and choose a card. No, wait, I'll stand at the other side of the room so that I can't peek. Don't forget to memorize your card. Now, spread them out on the table. Ahh! I am getting the impression of a red card, a high card, a royal card... the queen of diamonds!"

PERFORMANCE

1 Invite two members of the audience up and tell them they will be doing this trick themselves.

2 Tell the audience you are dividing the deck into two. Then split the deck into two halves (round-topped and flat-topped), and give one half to each of your two helpers.

3 Tell each of the two assistants to select one card from the other person's half-deck.

4 They should now look at the card they have chosen, show it to the rest of the audience, and memorize it. Make sure you can't see the cards they have chosen.

5 Now tell each of them to put their chosen card into their *own* half-deck and to shuffle their cards thoroughly.

6 Ask the helpers to spread out their half-decks on the table. You can now amaze both them and the audience by identifying the cards that they chose.

KINGS CHANGE

The audience sees four kings in your hand. You take the king of clubs and slide it down your arm—it turns into the ace of clubs! When you show the cards again, they are all aces.

PREPARATION

YOU WILL NEED:
- four kings, four aces, and any other three cards from the deck
- a ruler
- a pencil
- scissors
- glue

1 Glue the back of the king of clubs to the back of the ace of clubs.

2 Cut the other three kings and aces in half diagonally, from the top right to the bottom left corner. Glue the king of hearts half and the ace of hearts half to the *front* of one of the spare cards. Now do the same with the other two kings and aces.

Patter

"Here are four handsome kings...and here is the king of clubs by himself. I'd rather have a higher card....Oh look, here's the ace of clubs. What about these other three?...They've all become aces, too!"

PERFORMANCE

1 Show the audience that you are holding four kings in your hand.

2 Put the other cards facedown on the table, take the king of clubs, and place it against your arm. Hold it between your thumb and middle finger, as shown.

3 Allow the card to flick away from your middle finger and run it down your arm, turning it as you do so. The king will appear to change into the ace of clubs.

4 Pick up the other three cards and turn them the other way so that the ace halves are on top. Put the ace of clubs at the front, then show all four aces to the audience.

FEEL THE FORCE

This technique, known as "forcing a card," allows you to make someone pick the card you want them to. You'll need to practice handling the deck with your stronger hand, but it is a useful technique to learn.

PREPARATION

YOU WILL NEED:
• a deck of cards

SETUP

Put the card that you want someone to choose on the top of the deck. Make sure you memorize this card.

PERFORMANCE

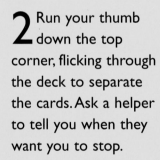

1 Hold the deck face-down in your right hand (if you are right-handed), with your thumb at the top corner.

2 Run your thumb down the top corner, flicking through the deck to separate the cards. Ask a helper to tell you when they want you to stop.

3 Using your left hand, open the deck like a book at the point where you've been told to stop.

4 Lift the top part of the deck between the tips of your left fingers and thumb. As you do this, use the fingers of your right hand to slide the top card off so it falls onto the lower part of the deck.

5 Offer your helper the lower part of the deck so that he or she takes the top card. This "chosen" card is the one you've already memorized.

SENSITIVE SOLE

Once you know how to "force" your helper to pick a card, there are a number of variations you can perform. In this trick, your helper picks a card "at random," puts it back into the deck, and shuffles the cards. The deck is thrown into the air, you walk over the cards, and the chosen card magically appears in your shoe!

PERFORMANCE

1 Force your helper to choose a card, using the technique described on page 31.

3 Ask him to give the cards a good shuffle before handing the deck back to you.

4 Throw the whole deck up into the air and let the cards land in a pile on the floor.

2 Ask your helper to memorize the card, then put it back into the deck.

Tips

If the chosen card lands faceup on the floor, you can change the emphasis of the trick as follows: walk over the cards, saying that your feet will tell you when they come into contact with the chosen card. Then bend over, pick up the card, and show it to the audience. As for a finale, say that shoes are not the only things that come in pairs, and bring out the identical card from inside your shoe.

SETUP

1. Put a card, identical to the one you are going to force your helper to choose, in your shoe.

2. Put the actual card your helper is going to choose at the top of the deck.

5 Walk over the cards on the floor, saying that you have sensitive feet.

6 Now stop at the point where you "feel" the card is and bend down to take off your shoe.

Patter

"Here's a feat of magic I have been walking on, I mean working on, for some time.... Choose a card, remember what it is, and we'll return it to the deck.... A good shuffle.... I'll throw the whole deck up into the air.... Now that they're on the ground, my feet should be able to feel your card.... Wow, the card has jumped off the floor and through my shoe! Gosh! Was this your card?!"

7 With a flourish, reveal that the chosen card is inside your shoe!

IN-JOG

This is a technique that allows you to keep track of a card that has been freely chosen by a member of the audience. The term "in-jog" refers to the card—positioned on top of the chosen card—that slightly sticks out toward you in the deck. By keeping the in-jog card under your control as you shuffle, you can always locate the chosen card.

PREPARATION

YOU WILL NEED:
• a deck of cards

PERFORMANCE

1 Ask your helper to select any card she likes.

2 Tell her to look at the card and memorize it.

3 She then puts her chosen card back on top of the deck.

4 Holding the deck in your left hand (if you are right-handed), slide half of the deck out from the bottom with your right hand. You are now ready to do the in-jog.

5 With your left thumb, slide the top card off the half-deck that is in your right hand. Make sure this card sticks out about 1/2 in. toward you.

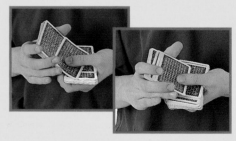

6 Now shuffle the rest of the cards in your right hand onto the half-deck in your left hand. Do this a little messily so the cards are not all neatly lined up.

Tips

1 You will need to practice this technique until the movements are smooth and undetectable. Watch the angle of your hands, so that the audience doesn't see the break.

2 To find out which card is the chosen one, fan the cards out toward you as if you were sorting them, and peek at the top card.

7 The deck is now in your left hand, with the chosen card under the card that is sticking out toward you (the in-jog card).

8 Turn the deck sideways in your left hand. With your right thumb, push the top half of the deck away from the bottom half, using the in-jog card.

selected card

9 You will now have a V-shaped break in the deck. The face-down card below the break is the one that your helper has chosen.

10 Shuffle all the cards above the break into your left hand.

11 Put the bottom half-deck, from below the break, on top of the other cards in your left hand. The top card is the chosen one.

12 Take the deck back into your right hand and shuffle it by sliding the top card off and putting it at the back of the deck.

13 Now shuffle the whole deck until you get to the last card, which you put back on top. You now know the chosen card is back on top.

LIE DETECTOR

You can perform this trick when you have mastered the in-jog technique described on pages 34–35. Your helper picks a card at random from the deck, which you then identify.

PREPARATION

YOU WILL NEED:
- a deck of cards

PERFORMANCE

I Ask your helper to pick any card from the deck.

2 Tell her to look at the card, memorize it, then put it back on the top of the deck.

3 Shuffle the deck using the in-jog technique (see pages 34–35). At the end, peek at the top card—this is the chosen card.

4 Now give the deck to your helper and ask her to shuffle it thoroughly.

5 Tell your helper to turn over the cards on the table one at a time. She should say, "That is not my card," even when she gets to the card she has picked.

6 Tell your helper that you will know from her voice whether or not she is lying. When she turns over her chosen card....

Patter

"I can tell just by the tone of your voice whether you are telling the truth. Pick a card, and I'll shuffle the deck...maybe I was cheating—you shuffle the cards....Deal them faceup, saying each time, 'That is not my card'....Ah, a little hesitation—that was your card."

7 ...tell her you know she is lying and point to the right card.

KEY CARD

This is another technique for finding out which card your helper has freely selected. It is similar to the in-jog technique (see pages 34–35), but it's much easier to learn and perform.

PREPARATION

YOU WILL NEED:
• a deck of cards

SETUP

Memorize the card at the bottom of the deck. This is the "key card."

Patter

"Pick a card. We have to lose it in the pack. Say 'stop' anywhere you like....Here? Put your card back in the pack....I can see a black card, a card with the number five—the five of clubs!"

PERFORMANCE

1 Ask your helper to pick any card from the deck. He should look at the card and memorize it.

2 Deal a few cards onto the table and ask your helper to say "stop" at any time.

3 Now tell him to put his chosen card on top of the pile on the table.

4 Put the rest of the cards on top. The key card is now on top of the chosen card.

5 Look at the cards as if you are concentrating, and slowly "guess" the chosen card. Or you can glance through the cards, see which one has been chosen, and perform a similar "guessing" trick, e.g., Lie Detector (see page 36).

TWICE AS RICE

In this impressive trick, the audience sees you fill an empty margarine tub to the brim with uncooked rice. You then place an identical margarine tub upside down over the top. When you take the top tub away, the rice has doubled in quantity.

PREPARATION

YOU WILL NEED:
- two identical empty margarine tubs with lids
- scissors
- glue
- tape
- a cup of uncooked rice
- a deep-sided tray
- colored paper or paints

1 Carefully cut around the lip of one of the margarine tub lids, leaving an edge so that it can be glued easily.

2 Glue the lid into one of the tubs, about halfway down.

3 Optional: decorate both tubs, but make sure they are identical.

Patter

"I am going to fill this tub with rice. Oops, too much, I just need to level it off with my wand....Now it is filled to the brim....You see here another tub—this one's empty....I'll put this second empty tub on top....Now I can show the rice and tubs to the frozen north... to the mysterious east... to the sunny south...and to the wild, wild west....And now that I've been all around the world...our rice may not be twice as nice, but it is twice as rice!"

PERFORMANCE

1 Fill the unaltered tub above the brim with rice.

2 Level off the rice with your wand, allowing any spillage to fall on the tray.

3 Take the lid off the second tub, keeping the open top away from your audience.

4 Place the changed tub upside down on top of the tub that is filled with rice.

5 Turn the tubs sideways, holding them firmly together, and show them to all four corners of the room.

6 When you turn to face your audience, turn the tubs upright onto the tray, making sure the altered tub is now at the bottom.

7 As you dramatically remove the top tub, the rice will spill out all over the tray. You have apparently doubled its volume.

CEREAL KILLER

You open up a box of cereal in front of the audience, but there is only one tiny cereal flake left inside. You demonstrate that the box is empty by opening the bottom and allowing the audience to look right through it. Then you close the bottom and the top and tap your wand on the box. When you open the top of the box again, you can pour a full portion of cereal into the bowl.

PREPARATION

YOU WILL NEED:
- two identical cereal boxes
- enough cereal to fill a bowl
- glue
- scissors
- Velcro
- a bowl
- a spoon

1 Open the flaps of both boxes. Cut a section out of one box, going from the bottom corner to a width of 1½ in. at the top.

2 Turn the section inside out and spread glue on its outside edges. Stick it firmly inside the uncut cereal box.

3 Cut two strips of Velcro and glue them to the bottom flaps of the box. Now close the box at the bottom and fasten.

SETUP

Pack the secret compartment tightly with cereal. Cover the cereal with one of the side flaps and try shaking the box—it must not rattle. If it does, pack it even more tightly with cereal. Then close the box.

Tips

When you open the box to pour out the single flake of cereal at the start of the trick, hold your fingers firmly over the side flap to hide the secret compartment and to keep it closed.

PERFORMANCE

1 Open the cereal box and pour the single cereal flake into the bowl. Look sad when you see that there is nothing left.

3 Close the flaps of the cereal box and tap the box with your magic wand.

4 Now open the top of the box and pour out a whole bowlful of cereal!

2 Open up the bottom flaps of the cereal box and, pointing the base toward the audience, show them that the box is completely empty.

THROUGH THE TABLE

Here's a vanishing trick that can be performed right under the eyes of your audience. It will take a little practice in front of a mirror to get the timing right, but you'll find that, once you've perfected it, this is a very effective trick that will impress your friends enormously.

PREPARATION

YOU WILL NEED:
- a saltshaker
- a paper napkin
- a small coin

PERFORMANCE

1 Put a coin on the table and tell the audience that you are going to push it right through the table.

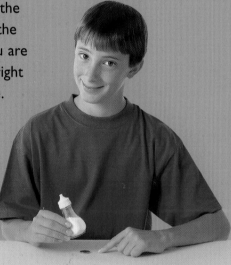

2 Put the saltshaker on top of the coin, then cover the saltshaker with the napkin "for safety reasons."

3 Place your hands on the napkin on either side of the saltshaker so that you have the saltshaker in your grip.

4 Tell the audience that after a count of three, the coin will go through the table. Now move the saltshaker, covered by the napkin, back and forth from its position on the table to a position just above your lap to see if the coin is gone.

5 Move the saltshaker back and forth three times, checking to see if the coin is still there. Click the saltshaker on the coin each time.

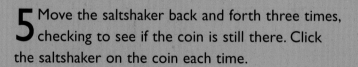

If you can't find a saltshaker with a pointed top, you can use another object that is similar in size and that tapers at the top.

Tips

As an extra element to this trick, you can reach under the table at the end of the trick—as if you are reaching for something on the floor—and bring the saltshaker up from your lap. Show the audience that it went right through the table.

6 On the fourth count, at the point where the saltshaker and napkin are above your lap, gently let the saltshaker drop into your lap and return the napkin, still holding its shape, to its original position above the coin.

7 Release the napkin and, before your audience realizes that the saltshaker is no longer there . . .

8 . . . bang your hand flat onto the napkin—the coin is still there, but the saltshaker is gone!

Patter

"I'm going to push this coin right through the table with this saltshaker....
It looks a little fragile, so we'll cover it with a napkin....
On the count of three, the coin should disappear. One ...two...three...Whoops! The coin is still there, but the saltshaker has disappeared."

BUSTED BANANA

By using a technique called "magician's choice," which allows you to make your helper choose the number you want him to, you can do this clever piece of magic. The audience watches as a banana is peeled and then falls into the same number of pieces as the number chosen by your helper.

PREPARATION

YOU WILL NEED:
- stiff paper or cardboard
- a thick pen
- scissors
- a bunch of bananas
- a darning needle

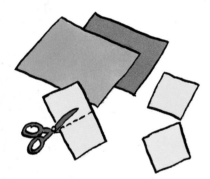

1 Cut out four pieces of cardboard. They should be about the same size as a playing card.

2 Write a number on each card. You can choose any numbers, but one of them must be a 3.

Patter

"Choose two numbers. Two and four? I'll remove these cards....Now another number. Three? Okay, I'll take away the card you didn't want....Now, banana, which number is left?... Sorry, can't hear you. Peel you? Why? Oh, all right...Ah, the answer is inside."

Tips

1 The banana can fall into three, four, or five pieces. Vary the number at different shows in case the same person sees it more than once.
2 For a stage show, use larger cards and an easel to display the numbers.

SETUP

Just before the performance (not too early, or the banana will turn brown), stick the darning needle into one of the bananas a third of the way from the top. Wiggle the needle gently from side to side. In the same way, make a second hole with the needle a third of the way from the bottom of the banana.

PERFORMANCE

1 Put the four cards faceup on the table, in no particular order. Then ask your helper to choose any two numbers.

4 If he has pointed to the 3, take away the other card. If he has not pointed to the 3, take away the card he has pointed to.

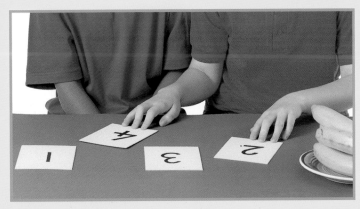

2 If your helper has not picked the 3, take away the two cards he has picked. If he has picked the 3 as one of his two cards, take the other two cards off the table. (You need to be left with the 3 on the table.)

5 Hand your helper a banana (the one you prepared earlier), and tell him the banana will know which number he has chosen.

6 Tell your helper to peel the banana. The banana will fall into three pieces.

3 Ask your helper to pick one of the two remaining cards. (Again, you need to be left with the 3 on the table.)

GLASS MAGIC

You need a member of the audience to participate in this trick. After showing your helper a coin at the bottom of a wineglass, ask him to cover the top of the glass while you tap his hand from underneath with a second coin. This coin will appear in the glass alongside the first coin.

PREPARATION

YOU WILL NEED:
- a bowl-shaped wineglass
- three coins, one large and two small (the small coins should be the same)

PERFORMANCE

I Slide a small coin, hidden beneath a larger coin, down the side of the glass.

3 Tilt the glass onto the palm of your helper's hand. Again, he will see only the larger coin.

2 Now swirl the glass to show that there is only one coin in it. The smaller coin should stay hidden under the larger one. Show your helper the "single" coin.

4 Now ask your helper to hold the glass upside down between his palms. Take the other small coin and tell the audience that it will work its way through your helper's hand and up into the glass.

SETUP

Make sure you have the right combination of glass and coins before you begin. Experiment by swirling two coins—the larger one above a smaller one—around the glass.

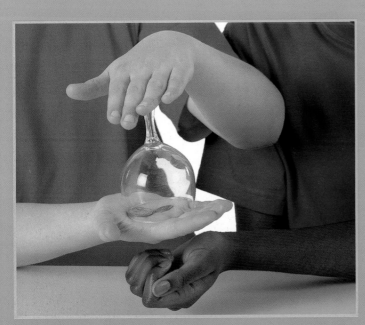

5 With the second small coin visible between your thumb and index finger, tap your helper's hand from below. The jolt will make the smaller coin hidden in the glass appear on top of the larger coin. Quickly hide the small coin that you were holding in your hand by dropping it into your closed palm and, from there, into your lap or your pocket.

ICE CREAM QUEEN

This trick starts with a member of the audience selecting one card from a deck. You then place the deck inside a cone made of folded paper. When the cone is opened up, the deck of cards has vanished, but when you turn the opened cone around, a large picture of the card chosen by your helper is stuck to the side.

PREPARATION

YOU WILL NEED:
- two squares of colored construction paper (12 in. x 12 in.)
- decorative tape
- glue
- a deck of cards
- a giant queen of hearts card

1 Tape together the two squares of colored paper, leaving a 5-in. opening in one corner.

2 Glue the large queen of hearts (or other chosen card) to the center of one side of the squares.

3 Make three folds in the squares, as shown. When folded up, this should make a cone.

Patter

"This is an audience participation trick. First of all, my friend will choose a card and show you what it is....Now she shuffles the deck—thank you—and I place the deck into this cone....Now, if you all shout 'jump,' the card my friend has chosen will jump out of the cone....Oops, that was a little too loud. The whole deck of cards has jumped out of the cone. No, there is nothing there...except for one card, that is. Was your card... the queen of hearts?"

PERFORMANCE

1 Use the forcing technique described on page 31 to make your helper pick the queen of hearts. She should show the card to the audience, then put it back anywhere in the deck.

3 Look into the cone and explain that when the audience shouted "jump," they scared away all the cards. Open the cone to show that the deck has vanished. (Keep the large card facing you.)

2 Ask your helper to shuffle the deck, then you drop it into the hidden pocket of the cone. It should look as if you are putting the deck into the middle of the cone.

4 With a smile, say there is just one card left and, turning the cone around, ask your helper if this was the card she picked.

LINKING SILKS

The vanishing cone (pages 48–49) is useful for making small objects appear and disappear. Using three cones, you can perform the following trick. You put three cones into three glasses. Then you put one silk scarf into each cone. When open up the first cone, the silk has vanished. The same thing happens when you open up the second cone. When you open up the third cone, though, you pull out all three silks linked together.

PREPARATION

YOU WILL NEED:
- six squares of colored paper, 12 in. x 12 in. (e.g., two green, two yellow, two blue)
- three tall, thin glasses in which to rest the cones
- six silks (two each of three different colors)

1 Tape two pairs of colored paper squares together, leaving a gap of 5 in. in one corner (see page 48).

2 Tape the third pair of squares together (the yellow pair is shown here), leaving two 5-in. gaps.

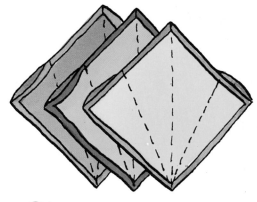

3 Make three folds in each of the squares as shown, then fold them into three cones.

SETUP

1 Tie three different colored silks together and put the three remaining silks to one side ready for use.

2 Feed the linked set of silks into one pocket of the yellow cone, leaving a tiny edge of the top silk sticking out.

3 Lay the three paper squares flat on the table.

PERFORMANCE

1 Take each square, fold it into a cone, and put one cone in each glass.

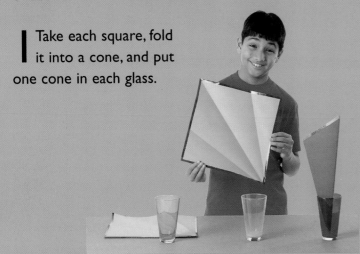

4 Open up the blue cone and show that the first silk has vanished. Open up the green cone and show that the next silk has vanished.

2 Put one silk into the secret pocket of the blue cone. To the audience, it should look as if you are putting the silk into the middle of the cone. Then put another silk into the green cone pocket.

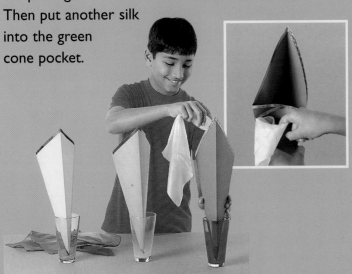

5 Hold the yellow cone firmly in the glass with one hand and, with the other hand, pull out the chain of linked silks.

3 Now put the third silk into the empty pocket of the yellow cone. At the same time, make sure the top edge of the linked set of silks (in the other pocket) is hanging over the edge of the cone.

DEVIL'S HANDCUFFS

Both ends of a piece of rope are tied snugly around both your wrists by one or two helpers. You then take a bracelet in one hand, and hide both hands and the bracelet under a large silk scarf. Seconds later, your helpers remove the scarf—and the bracelet is dangling from the rope!

PREPARATION

YOU WILL NEED:
- a piece of rope about 3 ft. long
- a large silk scarf
- two identical bracelets
- a long-sleeved top

SETUP

Slide one bracelet up your arm, hiding it under your sleeve.

PERFORMANCE

1 Ask two helpers to tie one end of a piece of rope around one wrist and the other end around the other wrist.

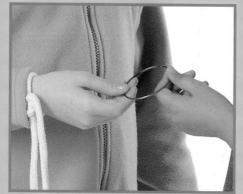

2 Ask one helper to pass you the bracelet, and tell the audience you will make this appear on the rope with your hands still tied.

Patter

"Can I have two volunteers who know how to tie a strong knot? Thank you.... Tie each end of this rope around my wrists—see, I've been handcuffed.... Now pass me that bracelet...and cover my hands with this scarf.... Now, here's a knotty problem. How can I get the bracelet on the rope without untying the knots?...On the count of three, take the scarf away.... One, two, three, magic!"

3 Tell your helpers to cover your hands with the scarf. They should hold up the ends of the scarf.

4 With your hands out of sight, put the bracelet in your pocket or under your clothes. Then slide the hidden bracelet down your sleeve on top of the rope.

5 Now ask your helpers to take the scarf away. Hold up your arms with a flourish and show the bracelet dangling from the rope.

Tips

1 For a close-up performance, slide the bracelet off your arm while it is under the table.
2 To prove the knots haven't been untied, ask a helper to mark the rope.

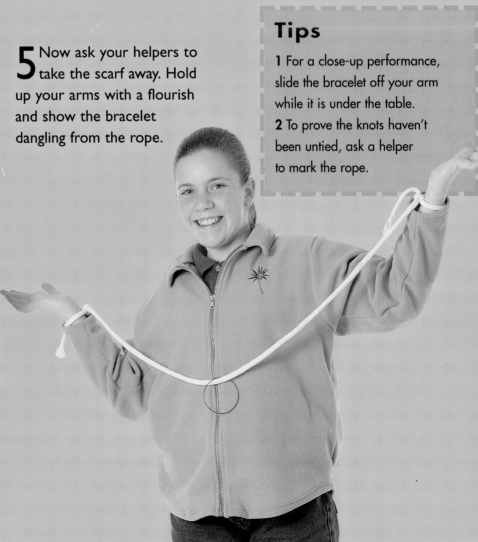

MIRROR BOX

The box described here is a handy prop that can be used for several appearing and vanishing tricks (see page 56 and pages 66–69). It has two compartments, but because of the mirror angled inside it, the audience only sees one. The other "invisible" compartment can be used to hide silks or other objects.

PREPARATION

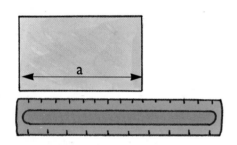

1 Measure the longest side of the mirror. This is measurement (a).

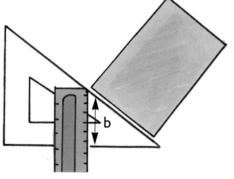

2 Hold the short side of the mirror against the long side of the triangle. Use a ruler to measure the drop. This is measurement (b).

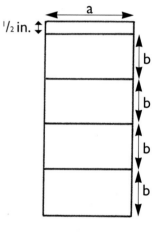

3 Draw two vertical lines on the cardboard. The distance between the lines should be the same as measurement (a). Draw a line across the top to join the vertical lines. Leave a gap of 1/2 in., then draw four more horizontal lines, each the width of (b) from the next one.

Tips

1 Get the mirror before making the box. It can be the size of a compact mirror (small enough to put in a purse). But if you are putting on a stage show, you will need a bigger box, so look for a mirror that measures about 6 in. x 8 in.

2 When you tell the audience what you are doing, remember not to refer to the box as a mirror box!

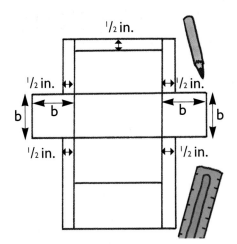

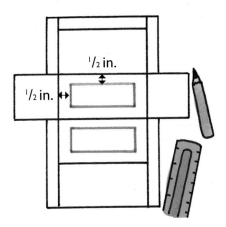

4 Draw a square on each end of the second rectangle from the top, as shown. Then draw a line 1/2 in. wide around the edges of the three remaining rectangles.

5 Draw a smaller rectangle inside each of the two central rectangles. The gap around the edge of the smaller rectangles should be 1/2 in. Cut around three sides of these rectangles, as shown here in blue.

6 Draw lines across the corners of the three large rectangles to mark the edges of the tabs. Now cut out your box following the blue dotted and black lines shown here. Score along the red lines using a ruler and a pair of closed scissors.

7 Fold up the sides and one end of the box and glue in the tabs. Then slide the mirror diagonally into the box and fold up the other end, gluing the tabs in place.

8 To help create the illusion of an empty box, it is a good idea to line the inside with striped paper. This is easiest to do after Step 4, before you use the scissors.

9 Now decorate your box. If you are using colored paper to decorate the outside, it is also best to do this after Step 4. Stick Velcro fasteners on the two doors.

MIRROR MAGIC

The audience sees you place four silks one by one into an empty box. When you pull them out, they are linked together.

PREPARATION

YOU WILL NEED:
- the Mirror box (pp. 54–55)
- eight silks (two each of four different colors)

SETUP

1 Tie four different-colored silks together and put them into the box through the door at the top.

2 Put the other four silks on the table, ready to use.

Patter

"You can see that this box has nothing in it.... One by one, I will put each of these silk scarves into the box.... Now for a little magic .... When I open the door, the scarves have joined forces!"

PERFORMANCE

1 Open the door at the front of the box and show the audience that there is nothing inside.

2 Put the first silk into the box through the front door.

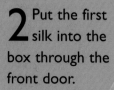

3 Now put the next three silks into the box one by one.

4 Close the box and wave your magic wand over it.

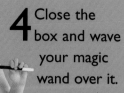

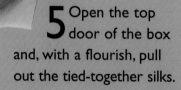

5 Open the top door of the box and, with a flourish, pull out the tied-together silks.

UP YOUR NOSE!

This trick works well in a stage setting. If you are feeling confident, you can perform it close-up. The audience sees you make a wand disappear halfway up your nose—or even into your ear! Follow the instructions below carefully.

PREPARATION

YOU WILL NEED:
- black construction paper
- white construction paper
- glue
- scissors

1 Roll up a piece of black paper to make a narrow tube about 6 in. long. Then stick down the edge.

2 Cut out a piece of white paper ¹/₂ in. x 2 in. Wrap it around one end of the tube and glue it in place.

3 Wrap more white paper (³/₄ in. x 2¹/₄ in.) around the other end. This must be loose enough to slide up and down. Glue down the edge.

PERFORMANCE

2 As you move the sliding white end up toward your nose, keep the protruding black end (shown here) hidden behind your hand.

1 Place the fixed end of the wand against your nose with the white hidden beneath your fingers. Keeping the other white end in view, slide it slowly up the tube.

Patter

"Do you know why they call a magic wand 'magic'? Because it has a great disappearing trick of its own...Now you see it...now you only see a little bit of it."

3 Slide the white end back to its starting position, take the wand away, and show that your nose and the wand are fine!

SHAKE THAT BOX

The audience sees you take a paper clip out of one of three matchboxes. Then you mix up the boxes and ask a helper to point to the one with the paper clip in it. You rattle the box, but there is no sound. Now you point to another matchbox. This rattles, and when you open it up, there is the paper clip! Each time you mix up the boxes, your helper picks the wrong box.

PREPARATION

YOU WILL NEED:
- four empty matchboxes
- four paper clips
- a rubber band
- invisible double-sided tape

SETUP

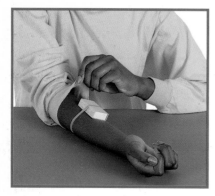

Put a paper clip into the fourth matchbox and attach this to your right arm with the rubber band. Then roll down your sleeve to hide the box.

Tips

You can do this trick as many times as you like—just remember to use the correct hand to shake the boxes!

PERFORMANCE

1 Open any box, take out the paper clip and show it to the audience and to your helper. Then put the paper clip back and close the box.

2 Shake the box you have closed with your right hand. The audience will hear the paper clip up your sleeve rattling and believe it is the one in the box.

3 Tell your helper to watch carefully while you move the matchboxes around several times.

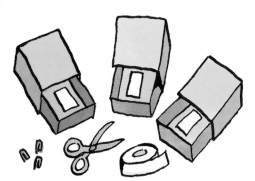

1 Stick some invisible double-sided tape to the bottom of three of the matchboxes.

2 Press a paper clip onto the tape. Make sure the boxes don't rattle when you shake them.

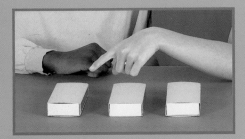

4 Ask your helper to point to the matchbox that she believes contains the paper clip.

5 Shake the matchbox that your helper pointed to using your left hand. There is no sound, and you tell her the box is empty.

6 Tell your helper that the paper clip is in another matchbox. Demonstrate this by shaking a matchbox of your choice, but make sure you use your right hand so that the paper clip rattles.

7 Now open up the matchbox you have just shaken and take out the paper clip from the bottom.

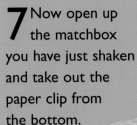

ANYONE HOME?

Here is a dramatic trick that works well if there is a lot of space between you and the audience. You will need a small, but cooperative assistant—a younger sister or brother, maybe—and you will need to spend time preparing the main prop—the house from which they will appear.

PREPARATION

YOU WILL NEED:
- a large cardboard box
- a pair of strong scissors
- glue
- colored cardboard or paint

Tips

When putting on a show, do this as an opening trick—little people can't sit still for long!

SETUP

1 Get your assistant to sit quietly under the table before anyone comes into the room. There should be a long tablecloth over the table, so she cannot be seen.

2 Place the roof right next to one side of the table, and put the main part of the house anywhere nearby.

PERFORMANCE

1 Pick up the house and show everyone that it is empty. Then put it down beside of the roof. There should be no space between the roof, the house, and the table.

2 Walk to the front of the stage and keep talking to your audience about what you are going to do next. Meanwhile, your assistant crawls from under the table, behind the roof, and through the secret door into the house. She must be very careful not to move the house as she does this.

1 Use a large cardboard box to make a house by removing the top and bottom. Cut gables at either end of the house.

2 Now make a roof out of cardboard. The roof must be detachable.

3 Decorate your house in any style you like.

4 Finally, cut a large door at the back of the house, leaving an edge of about an inch below the bottom of the door.

3 Pick up the roof and show the audience that there is nothing beneath it or between the house and the table. Then place the roof on top of the house.

4 You now say a few magic words or wave your wand.

5 As you take the roof off, wondering out loud whether anyone is home now, your assistant dramatically pops up out of the house.

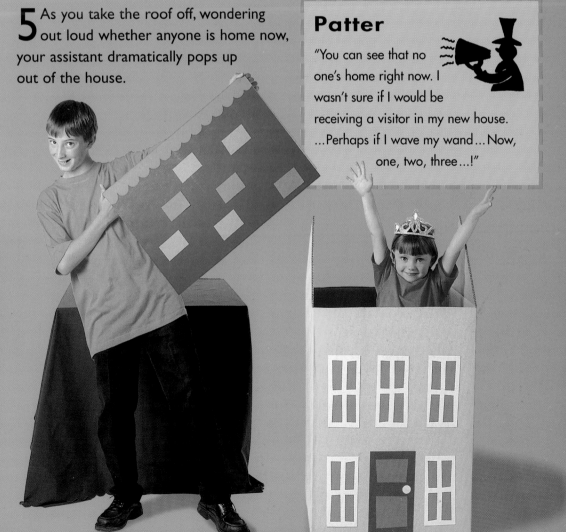

Patter

"You can see that no one's home right now. I wasn't sure if I would be receiving a visitor in my new house. ...Perhaps if I wave my wand...Now, one, two, three...!"

BIG BOX

In order to perform the trick on pages 64–65, you need to make the Big Box shown here. Before you start, think of who can help you perform the trick. This will help you decide how large the box needs to be.

PREPARATION

YOU WILL NEED:
- a cardboard box measuring approx. 20 in. x 30 in.
- two pieces of cardboard, approx. 20 in. x 30 in.
- a craft knife or strong scissors
- glue or tape
- colored paper or paint
- rope or strong tape for the handle

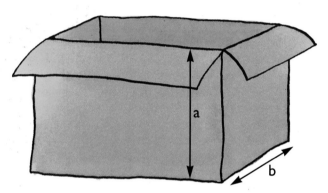

1 Find a large cardboard box that has square ends. In other words, its height (a) must be the same as its depth (b). It should be wider than it is tall.

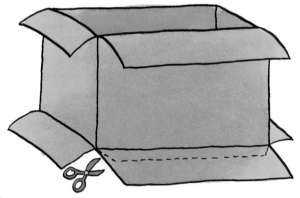

2 Open up the bottom flaps and cut off the two shorter flaps and one of the longer ones. Trim the remaining flap to approximately 1½ in.

Tips

1 This will be easier to make if you have two identical boxes. You can then cut the two pieces described in Step 4 from the second box.
2 When practicing this trick, make sure that your assistant will not be visible from anywhere in the audience.

3 Now paint the inside of the box black, including the flaps. Remember that the side with the 1½-in. flap will form the front of the box for your trick.

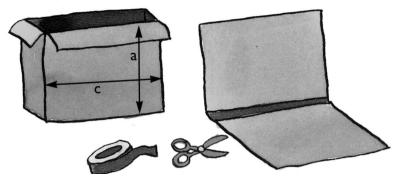

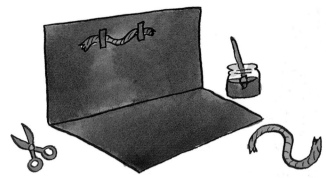

4 Now take the two pieces of cardboard and trim them to $\frac{1}{2}$ in. less than the width of the box (c) and $\frac{1}{2}$ in. less than the height of the box (a). Tape the two pieces together at right angles to each other.

5 Make a handle out of rope or tape, and attach it to the inside of the upper piece of cardboard, in the position shown. Paint the joined pieces of cardboard black on both sides.

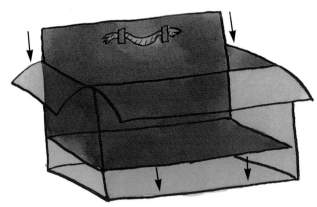

6 Slide the two pieces of cardboard into the box as shown. The side with the handle should be facing away from the front panel of the box. Where the two pieces of cardboard are joined, they should rest on the $1\frac{1}{2}$-in. flap.

7 Now decorate the outside of your box. You can leave it plain if you like, but you risk drawing attention to the painted flaps.

8 Finally, you should practice the following technique with your assistant: he sits on the false bottom of the box, holding on to the handle; you tilt the box forward and the false side (with the handle on it) now becomes the bottom of the box, with your assistant holding it in place.

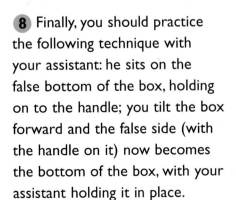

GET LOST!

This trick is an illusion that works well as an opening trick in a stage setting using the Big Box shown on pages 62–63. You will need an assistant—with whom you have practiced the trick—small enough to hide behind the box but old enough to work the box's magic door. The audience sees you open the box and tilt it forward to show it is empty. Then you close the box. When you open it again, your assistant magically appears.

PREPARATION

YOU WILL NEED:
- the Big Box (pp. 62–63)
- a solid table on which to perform the trick

PERFORMANCE

1 Open the box, tilt it forward, and show the audience that it is empty. (Your assistant sits behind it, holding the false bottom in place.)

2 Carefully tilt the box back onto the table. Your assistant pushes the false bottom forward and ducks into the box.

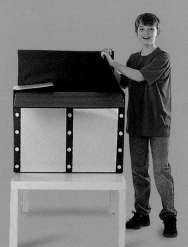

3 Now close the top flaps of the box.

SETUP

1 Practice tilting the box back and forth with your assistant holding on to the handle. He should be behind the box when it is tilted forward and inside it when it is standing on the table.

2 Before the audience comes in, get your assistant to sit inside the box, facing the front and holding on to the handle (see page 63).

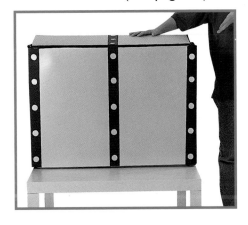

Patter

"What you see here is an empty box. Can everyone see? Empty on the inside, empty on the outside.... Now I'll close it up...and say a few magic words. Don't you think it would be fun to conjure up someone who could help me with the rest of my act?...Here we go again—I'll open up the box to see who or what appears....Here comes trouble!"

Tips

You can perform this trick at the beginning of your act, then work with your assistant during the show. To finish the act, you can reverse the trick by making your assistant climb back into the box and disappear!

5 Open the box without tilting it forward. Your assistant makes a dramatic appearance!

4 Say a few magic words over the closed box.

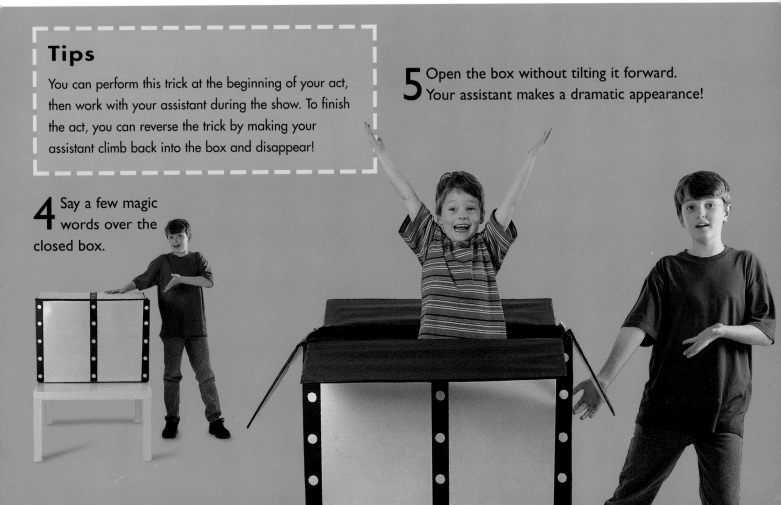

PUTTING ON A SHOW

There are several important things to consider when preparing for your show. From planning your routine to packing up your props, from setting up the stage to preparing your finale, there are a number of separate elements that will each require careful consideration well before the actual performance.

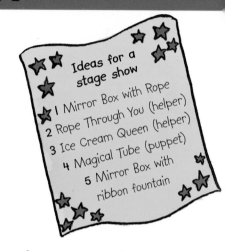

Ideas for a stage show

1 Mirror Box with Rope
2 Rope Through You (helper)
3 Ice Cream Queen (helper)
4 Magical Tube (puppet)
5 Mirror Box with ribbon fountain

PLAN YOUR ROUTINE

Choose the tricks you are going to perform ahead of time. The setting of your performance should be one of the first things you consider when deciding on your routine.

There are three suggested routines in this section. The one above is good for a stage setting, and the five tricks listed are photographed over the next four pages. Two more routines are shown on page 68—one for a floor show and one for a close-up performance.

Think about lighting, music, and how to display your props. A prompt card is useful to remind you of your routine.

PREPARING PROPS

Before you pack up your props, make sure you have carried out all of the PREPARATION steps and as many of the SETUP steps as you can do ahead of time. For example, if you are planning to make a ribbon fountain and a rope appear from the same Mirror Box, make sure you have packed the box with both objects in the right order. When packing, be careful how you arrange the props. Some are more fragile than others and may need careful packaging.

CHOOSE YOUR SPOT

Wherever your performance is going to be, it is important for you to familiarize yourself with the actual spot that will form your "stage" ahead of time. If it is in a room rather than on a stage, look for the room's natural focus. Think about where your audience can sit comfortably and have a good view.

SETTING UP

It is often a good idea to set up your "stage" with some extra lighting. Make sure the light doesn't come from directly behind you, because this will put you into shadow. If you are using music, think about what you are playing and what you will use to play it on. For both lighting and music, you will need access to an electric outlet. You may also need certain furniture props, such as a large table, perhaps with a long cloth over the top.

The magician uses the rope that he caused to appear in his opening trick as the main prop for the trick that follows.

MAKE AN IMPACT

Now that your audience is sitting comfortably, the lights are on, and the music is playing, it is time for the first trick of your act. Choose something visually dramatic— here the magician makes ropes appear from the Mirror Box.

NEXT....

Try to think of ways to make one trick flow smoothly into another. This can be done by using the prop that magically appeared in the previous trick. Here the magician uses the rope he conjured out of the Mirror Box for his next trick, Rope Through You.

YOUR HELPER

For some of the tricks you choose, you will need an assistant, or helper. Sometimes, this will be someone that you choose at random from the audience. When choosing a person to help you, pick out someone who looks genuinely willing to come forward.

Look for a willing volunteer to help you.

Not everyone wants to be in the limelight or run the risk of being caught off-guard. For certain tricks, your assistant will need to be someone who shares your knowledge of the trick and with whom you have practiced before the show. If your assistant is very young or is hiding in a tight corner somewhere, use them as soon as you can. Always be courteous to your helper—it is a mistake to make them look stupid for falling for the trick. Before they go back to their seat, thank them for participating in the show.

Below are two suggested routines. One is for a floor show and the other for a close-up show.

USING PUPPETS

To introduce some variety, you may decide to use a puppet to help you with your show. Pick a trick where you won't be hindered if you use a puppet on one of your hands, and practice the type of patter you and the puppet will use.

YOUR FINALE

For your final trick, try to finish on a dramatic note, so that you leave your audience wanting more. The trick shown here involves pulling a ribbon fountain out of the Mirror Box. (Make a ribbon fountain by laying a long ribbon in the box in a series of gentle zigzag folds). Be prepared to have one more trick ready just in case the audience asks for an encore. Whatever happens, don't be tempted to explain or repeat any of your tricks!

Puppets can be used to help your act along.

Producing a ribbon fountain from the box is a dramatic finale (right).

Ideas for a floor show

1 Anyone Home? (helper)
2 Devil's Handcuffs (helper)
3 Water Surprise
4 Twice as Rice
5 Linking Silks

Ideas for a close-up show

1 Busted Banana (helper)
2 Glass Magic (helper)
3 Number Crunching (helper)
4 Lie Detector (helper)
5 Through the Table

GLOSSARY

Magicians use a number of special words to describe their tricks and techniques. Below is a list of most of the new words you will come across, with an explanation of what they mean.

control A way of keeping track of a card that has been selected.

ditch To drop or lose something quietly and without being seen.

fake Something that looks normal but that has been adjusted to help you do a trick.

fanning powder (zinc stearate) A fine powder rubbed on playing cards so they are easier to handle.

finale The end of a trick or act.

forcing A way of making someone pick the card you want them to.

gimmick A secret piece of equipment.

illusion A trick that involves sawing people up or making them appear or disappear.

index The number and symbol in the corner of a playing card.

lapping Dropping something secretly into your lap.

levitation The illusion of someone or something floating without visible means of support.

load An object or objects produced from somewhere secret.

misdirection Any method used to make the audience look away while you are carrying out a move you don't want them to see.

move The actual execution of a secret movement.

palming Concealing an object in the palm of the hand.

patter The talk or description of a trick while performing.

production A trick where things are made to appear from thin air or empty boxes.

props Any equipment used to perform a trick.

pull A gimmick used to make an object vanish by pulling it up a sleeve or under a jacket.

routine The order of events in a trick or the order of tricks in a show.

setup A secret arrangement of equipment before the performance.

silk A silk scarf or piece of fine fabric of varying size.

sleight of hand An undetected movement of fingers to accomplish the moves of a trick.

square up To put cards into a neat pack.

steal To secretly remove something from where it is hidden.

switch To secretly exchange one thing for another.

talk An accidental clicking made by something hidden, which gives away its presence to the audience, e.g., the clicking of coins in a hand.

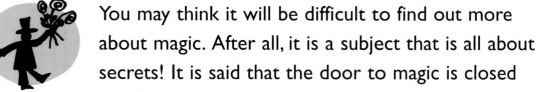

WHERE TO GO NEXT

You may think it will be difficult to find out more about magic. After all, it is a subject that is all about secrets! It is said that the door to magic is closed but not locked. Here are some ways of turning the handle.

LIBRARY

Look in your local library for information about magic—you will find books about its history, and containing new tricks you can learn.

MAGIC STORES

Many cities have magic stores. Look for them in your local phone book under headings like MAGIC STORES or MAGIC DEALERS.

MAGAZINES

Magic magazines can be very useful. Write for details of the following at the addresses below:

Magic
Stan Allen & Associates
7380 S. Eastern Avenue
Suite 124–179
Las Vegas, NV 89123

Abracadabra
Goodliffe Publications
150 New Road
Bromsgrove
Worcs B60 2LG
United Kingdom

MAGIC CLUBS

Large towns and cities often have a magic club. They may be more difficult to find than magic stores. If so, try phoning your nearest magic store and asking them how to find a local magic club. Many clubs have sections for younger members.

The most famous magic society in the world is The Magic Circle in London. It has a postal club for young magicians all over the world. Write to:
The Young Magicians' Club
The Magic Circle
12 Stephenson Way
London NW1 2HD
United Kingdom

THE INTERNET

On the Internet, there are probably more pages of information about magic and magicians than any other subject. Magicians are often as fascinated by computers as they are by magic!

FROM THE HORSE'S MOUTH

A good way to find out more about magic is to ask a visiting magician. But remember not to ask questions during a show!

INDEX

ACKNOWLEDGMENTS

Kingfisher would like to thank the following people for their invaluable help: the staff at the magic store Davenports for lending us equipment; Rachel Fuller for making the props; Marion McLornan for the special effects used in *Putting on a show*; Ray Moller and Sam Martin for their patience and expertise in the photographic studio; Jo Brown, Lisa Macdonald, and Katie Puckett for getting essential equipment. Finally, we would like to give a very big thank you to all the children who were our models: Aju Ahilan, Gurtaj and Janatpreet Bahd, Paul Bedford, Jay Briant, Tom Buddle, Antoine Campbell, Ben Clewley, Eleanor Davis, Cherelle Dovey (from Tiny Tots to Teens), Kaisha Esty, Thomas Gage, Connie Kirby (from the Scallywags agency), Kiki Loizou, Henry and James Moller, Ross Parsons, Claire and Nicholas Tolman.